Fox Stew 2

Fun at the Zoo

By Sandy Smith
Illustrated by Tiarra McCann

FOX STEW 2
Fun at the zoo

Copyright © Sandy Smith, 2021

All rights reserved. No part of this publication may be reproduced, stored in a retrieval system, or transmitted in any form or by any means, electronic, mechanical, photocopying, recording, or otherwise, without written permission of the author and publisher.

Published by: Sandy Smith, Chilliwack, B.C., Canada

Softcover ISBN: 978-1-77354-350-5
Hardcover ISBN: 978-1-77354-351-2

Publication assistance and digital printing in Canada by

PageMaster.ca

For Tiarra...Thanks for making this story come alive with your awesome artwork!

There once was a Fox who lived in a zoo,
and was learning to make vegetable stew.

He used to live near a small farm,
where the hens in the coop were kept cozy and warm.

When Fox was hungry he would go to the coop,
steal a fat hen and make chicken soup.

Then a very brave Hen made a sly plan,
and dragged the old fox onto a pan.

She tricked the old Fox and convinced him to hide,
found a large box and locked him inside.

Then Fox was shipped to a nice zoo,
and it was there that he learned to make vegetable stew.

Every night in the zoo, Fox was hungry and mad.
He could not sleep 'cause his belly was sad.

Sneaky old Fox wanted some meat,
and would creep out of his den to find something to eat.

Fox decided to sneak inside the food shack
to fill up his belly with a nice, tasty snack.

There were veggies and fruit, rice, wheat and beans,
but ham and salami could not be seen.

Fox nibbled a carrot and took a bite of a roll.
Still, he was left not feeling so full.

Where was the meat? This stuff tasted bad!
Fox wanted flavor. No meat made him sad.

Then under the counter Fox spotted a book.
Inside there were recipes so he took a look.

The pictures looked tasty; there were pies, soups and stew!
Maybe he'd try to make something new.

Fox got out a pan and started to fry.
The smell of carrots and onions made the Fox sigh.

Fox mixed in spices with herbs and tomatoes,
then added peppers, fresh dill and potatoes.

The pot began bubbling and smelled really yummy.
Fox had a taste and then rubbed his tummy.

It was delicious! Now Fox could sleep.
He snuck back to his cage without even a peep.

Each night Fox came back to make something to eat.
He learned to bake pies that were tangy and sweet.

Fox made salads and soups, appetizers and rices.
He made everything tasty with fresh herbs and spices.

Then animals started to notice sweet smells in the night,
And then saw the Fox sneak in before light.

They confronted the Fox so he showed them the shack.
Then the animals said, "Fox, make us a snack!"

"What would you like? Something salty or sweet?
Spicy or tangy?", then Fox turned on the heat.

The monkeys and tigers, elephants and apes,
all wanted Fox to make them some crepes.

Fox whipped up the eggs and flipped the crepes in the air.
He topped them with berries and served them with flair!

The animals loved them-they were delicious!
The finest ingredients made food nutritious.

Then the zookeeper noticed that things were not right.
The food in the fridge was now out of sight.

So, he hid in the kitchen and when nighttime came,
he watched the Fox cook-this was insane!

Then the animals came and filled up their bellies.
It looked like the shack had become quite a deli.

The zookeeper jumped out from his hiding spot
and said to the Fox, "Make me something hot."

Fox whipped up some soup that smelled mighty fine.
The zookeeper sat down, ready to dine.

Then he had an idea; the zoo could have a café.
There, Fox could cook all night and all day.

The people all came to the café at the zoo.
They enjoyed every bit of the soup, pie and stew.

The café was a success 'cause Fox had a gift:
With fine food he could give others a lift.

Now Fox began to feel something new,
He enjoyed serving others and inside his heart grew.

He remembered the hens who he treated so bad.
For all he had done, he began to feel sad.

Then Fox had an idea-he knew what to do!
He got out a pen and a paper, or two.

He wrote a note to the hens in the coop.
It started with "Dear hens, do you like soup?"

"You all are invited to the café at the zoo,
where you will be treated to a sandwich or two."

"Please come, dear hens and visit the Fox,
who you tricked into hiding inside a large box."

The hens decided to see Fox at the zoo.
They would have soup and a sandwich, or two.

Waiting there was the Fox when they arrived.
He bowed before them; they were surprised!

The Fox seated the hens at tables beautifully set.
He served them the finest of food he could get.

There were salads and soups, appetizers and sweets.
Flavored with spices and herbs, and made without meat.

The finest of food Fox fed the hens.
Everything that they tasted was a ten out of ten.

The hens were impressed; Fox really had changed.
They cheered and thanked him for what he arranged.

Sneaky sly Fox was now kind-hearted and good.
He was a talented chef; proud he now stood!

Fox had come a long way from his days in the den,
all because of a plan of a very brave Hen.

One day the papers arrived and took Fox's picture.
He smiled for the cameras while he whipped up a mixture.

Other books by Sandy Smith

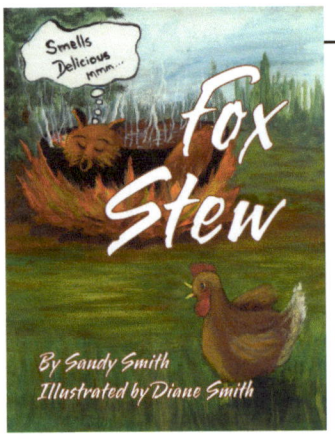

Fox Stew

This is a story of a fox and a hen,
The fox was a bully, so he left his den...
And made the mistake of hunting the flock,
But this hen was so clever! She lived under no rock!

She tricked him and flicked him and cooked him in stew,
"Now you know better than to mess with my crew!"
For anyone having trouble with hungry mean foxes,
Just remember: it's best when they're locked up in boxes!

ISBN: 978-1-988048-52-9 (paperback)

I Want More!

How many presents will it take to make this Princess smile? The frustrated King and Queen are about to find out. Join this young princess in her journey of self discovery, teaching her the value of friendship, love and giving.

ISBN 978-1-988048-24-6 (6x8 version)
ISBN 978-1-988048-39-0 (9x12 version)

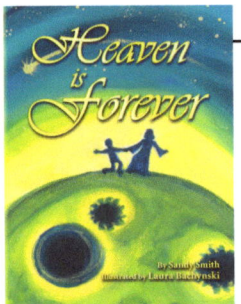

Heaven is Forever

Heaven is Forever is a story of hope, reminding us that there is much to look forward to and experience when our life on earth is through. Join in the journey as a young child and his friends experience endless adventures and special moments in Heaven.

ISBN 978-1-988048-19-2 (6x8 version)
ISBN 978-1-988048-18-5 (9x12 version)

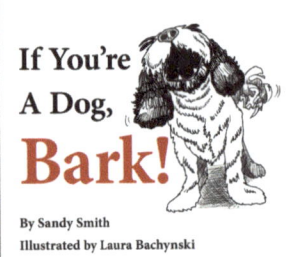

If you're a Dog, Bark!

A delightful story about a dog who wants to meow just like a cat. He likes to chase birds, take long naps and drink warm milk, so he must be a cat! Find out if this charming puppy succeeds in his quest to meow.

ISBN 978-1-988048-20-8 (6x6 version)
ISBN 978-1-988048-34-5 (9x9 version)

About the Author

Sandy Smith has been an educator for over 20 years and is passionate about creating stories and poems with messages of hope, redemption and love. Her published works include: *Heaven is Forever*, *If You're a Dog, Bark!*, *I Want More!* and *Fox Stew*.

About the Illustrator

Tiarra McCann is a self taught artist with a passion for animals, nature, and telling stories through her artwork. Tiarra works with a variety of mediums, but primarily focuses on digital art. She also enjoys animating, making videos, and petting cats. *Fox Stew 2* is the first book she has illustrated and she is looking forward to future projects.

https://pagemasterpublishing.ca/by/sandy-smith/

To order more copies of this book, find books by other
Canadian authors, or make inquiries about publishing
your own book, contact PageMaster at:

PageMaster Publication Services Inc.
11340-120 Street, Edmonton, AB T5G 0W5
books@pagemaster.ca
780-425-9303

catalogue and e-commerce store
PageMasterPublishing.ca/Shop

www.ingramcontent.com/pod-product-compliance
Lightning Source LLC
Chambersburg PA
CBHW040017050426
42451CB00002B/13